# A Sibling's Guide to

WRITTEN BY IRENE KIM     ILLUSTRATIONS BY SUMI KIM

To **Skylar**

my baby sister, always and forever

# "NORMAL"

It's okay to want a "normal" brother sometimes.
I've thought about it countless times too.
To be honest, I used to be jealous
of other twins and their "normal" interactions
like biking to school and playing games together
or bickering over, well, anything really
because I was never able to have that relationship.

But in the end, your unique experience will help you grow
in ways that you never expected.

# EXPLAINING

It can be hard to explain our brother to friends,
even when you want to and even when you don't.
Just know that you have the right to choose
whether to tell someone or not.
There is never a wrong choice.

"Do you have any siblings?"
"Yeah, I have a brother and a sister."
"Younger or older?"
"I actually have a twin brother and a younger sister."
"That's so cool! Does he go to this school? what's his name?"
"He's actually a grade below us because he held back
a grade, but his name is Minjae."
"Oh okay nice."

# PACE

Our brother lives life at his own pace
and you will learn more than you imagined by walking with him.
He will stop to sit at every bench,
drink out of every water fountain,
and walk on all the ledges.
We always plan our vacations to be at his pace—
to be just a couple days longer.
From him, you will learn how to slow down
and appreciate every moment.

# VOLUME

Our brother can be too loud sometimes.
Most days will be okay,
but other days might be harder to handle.
I came to better understand him once I realized
what comes naturally to us does not come naturally to him
and sometimes, raising his voice is the only way
for him to express his frustration.
But don't worry, there are more good days than bad.

# LUCKY

Always remember that we're lucky to live where we live—
where people are accepting and understanding
(at least, for the most part).
Back in fifth grade, my class read a book about autism and I mustered up
the courage to tell my classmates about our brother.

"He's a little different from us and it takes him longer to learn certain things, but there are also a lot of things he's really good at. He's really good at ice skating and playing video games."

My classmates were quick to understand and one of them even said:

"He could totally be a professional ice skater!"

I didn't realize it then, but looking back now, I recognize how lucky I was to have gotten such a positive response.

# PEOPLE

I've met some of the kindest people in the world thanks to our brother.
Teachers, aides, friends—sometimes even strangers.

These people are special because they help you realize that
the world is a much kinder place than you might think.

"SIMPLE"

Simple things aren't always so simple.
In fact, simple things are often the most difficult

Like dining out,
watching movies,
riding airplanes,
and eating different foods.
Even family gatherings and playdates.

It can be tiring, but accomplishing these
simple tasks will become a thousand
times more valuable.

# MISSING

You might miss out on what other people take for granted,
like having both parents at an important event.
Dad came alone to all of my high school lacrosse games
and my first-ever Carnegie Hall performance.
Mom came alone to all of my orchestra concerts.
It may seem unfair, but remember that
you will always have someone next to you—
whether it be Mom, Dad, or me—no matter what.

# ATTACHMENT

Learn to let things go—
you'll find that it's easier that way.

I learned the hard way when he ripped my favorite poster,
a week after I got it.
From that day on, I learned to let go of what cannot be helped.

# GAINING

Don't worry, there is so much you gain as well
like fast passes at amusement parks.
You'll also get to experience what others may never experience
like an indoor rock climbing wall
and tire swing in our very own garage
or getting to ice skate every Sunday morning for ten years.
These new experiences will help you
view the world with an open mind.

# FAULT

In the end, it's really no one's fault.
Not yours, not mine, not his.
And I believe you will grow from it all
—the good days and the bad days—
to find your truest self.

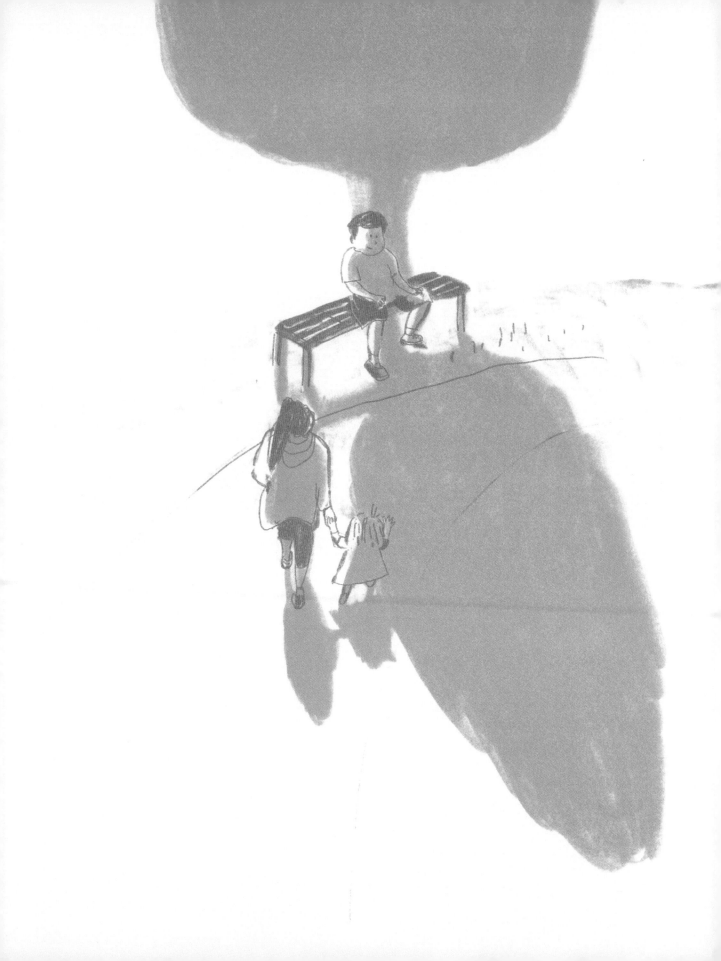

# Acknowledgements

Special thanks to Sumi gomo (수미 고모), the best illustrator and aunt, for bringing my story to life. None of this would have been possible without her because the book could very much have come out looking like the pictures down below and I can't express how grateful I am for her willingness to help.

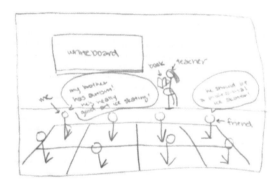 

And, as always, I would like to send a big thank you to Mom, Dad, Minjae, and Skylar for always supporting me and making me smile.

# Why I wrote this book

During the pandemic, I inevitably had to spend every second of every day with both Minjae, my twin brother, and Skylar, my one-year-old sister. As fun as it was, there were times when it was hard for all of us. So with everything cancelled and more time on my hands than I thought was possible, I began to think of ways that I could help ease Skylar into our ever-changing world.

Through my past volunteering experience, I had various opportunities to talk with both younger and older siblings of individuals with disabilities, and came to realize that we all had the same basic joys and frustrations in our day-to-day lives. At the time, the siblings who were older than me gave advice for the future and as we continued to talk, I began to realize how helpful it would have been to have someone older to guide me through the ups and downs. I wrote this book in hopes that I could be the older sister that I never had—for Skylar and for any other sibling out there who wants to be understood.

Printed in Great Britain
by Amazon